Foreword

Battered child syndrome is a tragic and disturbing phenomenon. Unfortunately, it is a crime that is often successfully hidden by its perpetrators. Law enforcement has an important role to play in uncovering cases of battered child syndrome and gathering evidence for their successful prosecution.

This guide contains practical information on the circumstances that point to the willful rather than the accidental injury or death of an infant or child and the specific evidence required to prove it. It places special emphasis on obtaining an expert medical examination, immediately documenting the injuries through photographs, and collecting and preserving physical evidence. The guide also shows investigators how their interviews with caretakers, family members, neighbors, school personnel, and others can shed light on the treatment the child has received over time and produce witnesses who can corroborate or refute suspected abuse.

Many jurisdictions are beginning to develop training programs to help police investigate this crime more effectively. This guide is an important contribution to this end and will aid child protection personnel and others in a position to identify, investigate, and prosecute cases of battered child syndrome.

Original Printing August 1996

Second Printing July 1997

Third Printing March 2000

Fourth Printing December 2002

NCJ 161406

I nvestigators should have a working knowledge of battered child syndrome and what it means to an investigation. Battered child syndrome is defined as the collection of injuries sustained by a child as a result of repeated mistreatment or beating. If a child's injuries indicate intentional trauma or appear to be more severe than could reasonably be expected to result from an accident, battered child syndrome should be suspected. In such cases, an investigator must do more than collect information about the currently reported injury. A full investigation requires interviewing possible witnesses about other injuries that the child may have suffered, obtaining the caretakers' explanation for those injuries, and assessing the conclusions of medical personnel who may have seen the victim before.

The issue of whether information on the victim's prior injuries or medical conditions will be admissible at a trial should be left to the prosecutor. However, an investigator's failure to collect such information leaves the prosecutor without one of the most important pieces of corroborative evidence for proving an intentional act of child abuse. Evidence of past inflicted injuries also may be the only information available to help the prosecutor distinguish between two or more possible perpetrators in the current case, and may help refute claims by the child's parents or caretakers that injuries suggestive of physical abuse were caused by an accident.

Critical Steps in Investigating Battered Child Syndrome

Investigators confronted with a case of possible child abuse or child homicide must overcome the unfortunately frequent societal attitude that babies are less important than adult victims of homicide and that natural parents would never intentionally harm their own children. When battered child syndrome is suspected, investigators should always:

* Collect information about the "acute" injury that led the person or agency to make the report.

* Conduct interviews with the medical personnel who are attending the child.

* Review medical records from a doctor, clinic, or hospital.

* Interview all persons who had access to or custody of the child during the time in which the injury or injuries allegedly occurred. **Always interview the caretakers separately—joint interviews can only hurt the investigation.**

* Consider any statements the caretakers made to anyone concerning what happened to the child who required medical attention.

* Conduct a thorough investigation of the scene where the child was allegedly hurt.

Interviews With Medical Personnel

The investigator must contact all medical personnel who had contact with the family, such as doctors, nurses, admitting personnel, emergency medical technicians (EMT's), ambulance drivers, and emergency room personnel:

* Talk with those who provided treatment for the child about what diagnoses and treatments were used. The attending physician will often be able to express at least an opinion that the caretakers' explanation did not "fit" the severity of the injury. **Failure to obtain an opinion from the attending physician should *not* end the investigation.**

* Speak with any specialists who assisted the attending physician.

* Have someone knowledgeable about medical terms translate them into laypersons' terms so that the exact nature of the injuries is clear.

* Obtain available medical records concerning the injured child's treatment, including records of any prior treatment. **Note:** If only one caretaker is suspected of abuse, the nonabusive caretaker may need to sign a release of the records. If both are suspected, most States have provisions that override normal confidentiality rules in the search for evidence of child abuse. Procedures for obtaining these records must be confirmed in each State.

* Interview the child's pediatrician about the child's general health since birth and look for a pattern of suspected abusive injuries.

It is absolutely vital that photographs of the child be taken as soon as possible after the child has been brought to the treatment facility. Most clinics and hospitals have established procedures for photographing injuries in obvious cases of abuse, but when the injuries are more subtle, they may overlook the need for photographs. The investigator should make sure that the medical personnel take and preserve photographs or that the investigating team takes them.

In a child homicide investigation, an autopsy must be performed. Most States mandate that such autopsies be performed when the death of any child under a certain age is undetermined or suspicious. In States without such a statutory mandate, the medical examiner or local prosecutor often has the authority to order an autopsy. This authority should be used whenever there is an unexplained death of a child.

Other Important Sources of Information

* Interview siblings, other relatives, neighbors, family friends, teachers, church associates, and others who may know about the child's health and history. People who surround the child and are part of his or her life are sometimes overlooked as sources of background information for a child abuse or homicide prosecution.

* Review EMT records or 911 dispatch tapes. These records are frequently overlooked and can be a valuable source of information. Families with more than one emergency may in fact be abusing children and may not just be hit by a long streak of "bad luck."

* Once the family history is obtained, request any police reports that may be held by law enforcement agencies in the jurisdiction where the family lives. Also check the child welfare agency's files on the family.

* Collect additional family history concerning connections between domestic violence and child abuse, substance abuse and child abuse, and other such connections, even apparently unrelated arrests or charges. These records may be helpful in piecing together the complicated picture of what happened to the child this time and who was responsible.

Consultation With Experts

Identifying experts is as important to the child abuse investigator as identifying and cultivating street informants in other types of investigations. If the investigator does not have a basic knowledge of the causes of young children's injuries, experts may be difficult to identify. Attending training conferences can provide the investigator with a great deal of basic knowledge and help establish a network of experts.

Interviews With Caretakers

A major trait of abusive caretakers is either the complete lack of an explanation for critical injuries or explanations that do not account for the severity of injuries. The investigation must not be dictated solely by caretakers' early explanations, because once they learn those do not match the medical evidence, they will come up with new ones.

In child homicide cases, for example, investigators will learn quickly about "killer couches," "killer stairs," and "killer cribs." Abusers frequently use these items in their explanations of a child's death. However, studies show that children do not die in falls from simple household heights; they do not even suffer severe head injuries from such falls.

In nearly every case of actual abuse, the caretakers will not be consistent in their explanations of the injuries over time. Sometimes the changes are apparent from statements abusers have made to others. Additional interviews may be needed to document the changing explanations and to follow up on additional information that the investigation uncovers.

Crime Scene Investigation

Caretakers' changes in explanations often mean investigators must visit the home or the scene of the injury more than once. The ideal time to obtain such evidence is immediately after the

Investigator's Checklist for Interviewing Caretakers

Investigators should ask the following questions to ensure a thorough interview with the caretakers.

❑ When did the caretakers first notice the child was ill or injured, and what exactly did they observe? What do they believe caused the illness or injury?

❑ Who was with the child at the time of the injury or when the child first appeared ill? (Cover as much time as possible up to 3 to 5 days.)

❑ What was the child's apparent health and activity level for the same period up to the time of the illness? Exactly how did the symptoms develop?

❑ What is the child's health history since birth?

❑ Has the child been hospitalized or treated for prior injuries or illnesses? If so, what treatment was needed or what caused those injuries?

❑ Which caretaker normally disciplines the child, and what form of discipline is used?

❑ What is the health of other children in the family?

❑ Who is the family doctor or the child's pediatrician?

❑ Does the child attend school or day care? Who is the child's teacher (or teachers)?

❑ Has the child shown any recent behavioral changes that are otherwise unexplained?

❑ If the nature of the current injuries is known, how do the caretakers explain what caused such injuries? If no explanation is given, were there times when the child was unsupervised or in the company of others?

❑ What is the child's developmental level? (Children who can barely crawl around cannot injure themselves by falling from a two-story building.)

child's injury is reported, before caretakers have an opportunity to tamper with the scene.

If the caretakers do not consent to a search of the scene, a search warrant may be necessary. The strongest evidence of the need for such a warrant will be the medical evidence of what probably happened to the child and the caretakers' inconsistent or absent accounts of the events.

Whatever explanation caretakers offer for the child's injury or injuries, it is vital that the investigator secure physical evidence. Be thorough in obtaining photographic evidence of the location where the injury took place. Physical evidence and records that must be preserved include:

* The crib from which the child allegedly fell.

* The child's "environment," including bedding within the bed or crib and other beds in the home.

* Any toys or objects the child allegedly landed upon.

* In cases where the child was apparently burned, a record of any sinks, bathtubs, and pots or pans containing water. In addition to testing the temperature of the standing water, test the temperature of water from the water heater and from each tap. Check the temperature setting of the water heater. This may help disprove an allegation that the child accidentally turned on the hot water. Other sources of heat in the home should be documented, regardless of the caretakers' initial explanation of what burned the child.

* A complete photographic or videotaped record of the home or other location in which the injuries allegedly occurred. Focus on areas that the caretakers already have identified as the site of the particular trauma (i.e., stairs, beds or crib, or bathtub).

Investigators should be trained by their local crime laboratory personnel on the types of evidence that can and should be processed and preserved in these cases:

* If the child apparently suffered cigarette burns, collecting cigarette butts found in the home may facilitate analysis of the burn patterns.

* If the case involves a combination of sexual and physical abuse, collecting the child's clothing and bedding may allow identification of what happened and who was involved.

* If the child shows evidence of bite marks, saliva swabbing should be done to allow positive identification of the biter.

* If the child has suffered a depressed skull fracture, any objects the approximate size of the fracture should be seized for appropriate analysis.

Investigative Guidelines for Child Homicides

It is not always readily apparent that a child's death was the result of homicide. In some cases, homicide is evident:

* It is fairly obvious that the child's death was caused by an abusive injury.

* The person who had custody of the child at the time the abusive injury was inflicted is known. Most infant deaths occur when the baby is in the care of known individuals.

* The injuries themselves are obviously the result of a deliberate intent to do harm — that is, there is really no debate that someone abused the child and that the abuse caused the child to die. Such cases include strangulation, beating, severe inflicted burns, such as scalding, and the use of a weapon.

Unfortunately, the more careful and planned out the killing is, the less likely it is that a medical explanation for the death will be found. Most fatal injuries resulting from abuse are much more subtle than poisoning, beating, bludgeoning, shooting, or strangulation. Suffocation, for example, often leaves absolutely no medical sign of the cause of death. Most infant deaths are related to head injuries, some of which leave no external sign of trauma.

In case after case of suspicious deaths of children, the caretakers' explanation is: "She fell off the couch (chair, changing table, or bed, or down the stairs)." Investigators must be aware that **children do not die of simple falls.** When investigating whether a child's death was a homicide, investigators must ask themselves the following questions:

* How do we find out what actually did happen to the child?

* How do we make sure we are talking to the right expert about what could have caused the child's death?

* How do we know we have talked to everyone who might be able to shed light on a difficult case?

When presented with a child who has died under suspicious circumstances in which there is no obvious sign of abuse, investigators should ask an experienced pediatrician to help locate a specialist whose medical expertise can help make sense of a confusing picture. However, everyone who handles child fatalities must have a basic understanding of the following conditions:

* Shaken baby syndrome.

* Munchausen syndrome by proxy.

* Sudden infant death syndrome (SIDS).

Shaken Baby Syndrome

The classic medical symptoms associated with infant shaking are:

* Retinal hemorrhage (bleeding in the back of the eyeball), often bilaterally (in both eyes).

* Subdural or subarachnoid hematomas (intracranial bleeding, most often in the upper hemispheres of the brain, caused by the shearing of the blood vessels between the brain and the dura mater or the arachnoid membrane).

* Absence of other external signs of abuse (e.g., bruises), although not always.

* Symptoms including breathing difficulties, seizures, dilated pupils, lethargy, and unconsciousness.

According to all credible studies in the past several years, retinal hemorrhage in infants is, for all practical purposes, conclusive evidence of shaken baby syndrome in the absence of a good explanation. Good explanations for retinal hemorrhage include:

* A severe auto accident in which the baby's head either impacted something with severe force or was thrown about wildly without restraint during the crash.

* A fall from several stories onto a hard surface, in which case there are usually other signs of trauma, such as skull fractures, swelling, intracranial collection of blood, and contusions.

Simple household falls, cardiopulmonary resuscitation (CPR), and tossing a baby in the air in play are not good explanations for retinal hemorrhage. There simply is not enough force involved in minor falls and play activities to cause retinal hemorrhage or the kinds of severe, life-threatening injuries seen in infants who have been shaken.

In most cases of shaken baby syndrome, there are no skull fractures and no external signs of trauma. The typical explanation given by the caretakers is that the baby was "fine" and then suddenly went into respiratory arrest or began having seizures. Both of these conditions are common symptoms of shaken baby syndrome.

The shaking necessary to cause death or severe intracranial injury is never an unintentional or nonabusive action. These injuries are caused by a violent, sustained action in which the infant's head, which lacks muscular control, is violently whipped forward and backward, hitting the chest and shoulders. The action occurs right in front of the shaker's eyes. Experts say that an observer watching the shaking would describe it as "as hard as the shaker was humanly capable of shaking the baby" or "hard enough that it appeared the baby's head would come off." In almost every case, the baby begins to show symptoms such as seizures or unconsciousness within minutes of the injury being inflicted. The baby may have difficulty in breathing, or breathing may stop completely. Often, but not always, when shaking causes death or severe injuries, it has been followed by sudden deceleration of the action caused by throwing the child down onto a surface that may be either soft or hard.

Shaken baby syndrome occurs primarily in children 18 months of age or younger. It is most often associated with infants less than a year old, because their necks lack muscle control and their heads are heavier than the rest of their bodies. An infant cannot resist the shaking, but a toddler can, to some extent. Although the collection of injuries associated with shaken baby syndrome is sometimes seen in toddlers, it is rare and is always a sign of extremely violent and severe action against the child.

Munchausen Syndrome by Proxy

Munchausen syndrome is a psychological disorder in which the patient fabricates the symptoms of disease or injury in order to undergo medical tests, hospitalization, or even medical or surgical treatment. To command medical attention, patients with Munchausen syndrome may intentionally injure themselves or induce illness in themselves. In cases of Munchausen syndrome by proxy, a parent or caretaker suffering from Munchausen syndrome attempts to bring medical attention to themselves by injuring or inducing illness in their children. The parent then may try to resuscitate the child or to have paramedics or hospital personnel save the child. The following scenarios are common occurrences in these cases:

* The child's caretaker repeatedly brings the child for medical care or calls paramedics for alleged problems that cannot be medically documented.

* The child only experiences "seizures" or "respiratory arrest" when the caretaker is there — never in the presence of neutral third parties or in the hospital.

* When the child is hospitalized, the caretaker turns off the life-support equipment, causing the child to stop breathing, and then turns everything back on and summons help.

* The caretaker induces illness by introducing a mild irritant or poison into the child's body.

Investigative guidelines in suspected cases of Munchausen syndrome by proxy

* Consult with all experts possible, including psychologists.

* Exhaust every possible explanation of the cause of the child's illness or death.

* Find out who had exclusive control over the child when the symptoms of the illness began or at the time of the child's death.

* Find out if there is a history of abusive conduct toward this child.

* Find out if the nature of the child's illness or injury allows medical professionals to express an opinion that the child's illness or death was neither accidental nor the result of a natural cause or disease.

* In cases of hospitalization, utilize covert video surveillance to monitor the suspect. Some cases have been solved in this way.

* Determine whether the caretaker had any medical training or a history of seeking medical treatment needlessly. Munchausen syndrome by proxy is often a multigenerational condition.

Sudden Infant Death Syndrome

Sudden infant death syndrome (SIDS) is not a positive finding; rather, it is a diagnosis made when there is no other medical explanation for the abrupt death of an apparently healthy infant. When a baby dies from shaking, intracranial injury, peritonitis (inflammation of the peritoneum, that is, the membrane that lines the abdominal cavity), apparent suffocation, or any other identifiable cause, SIDS is not even considered a possibility. SIDS rarely occurs in infants older than 7 months and almost never is an appropriate finding for a child older than 12 months.

A SIDS death is not a homicide, and apparent SIDS cases must be approached with great sensitivity. However, before SIDS can be ruled the cause of death, the investigator must ensure that every other possible medical explanation has been explored and that there is no evidence of any other natural or accidental cause for the child's death.

An investigator's suspicions should be aroused when multiple alleged SIDS deaths have occurred under the custody of the same caretaker. Statistically, the occurrence of two or three alleged SIDS deaths in the care of the same person strongly suggests that some degree of child abuse is involved. Whenever there is evidence that the child who has died was abused, or that other children in the family have been abused, SIDS is not an appropriate finding.

Even when there is no affirmative medical finding of the cause of death, prosecution may still be possible. In some circumstances, experts can explain what occurs when a child is suffocated and can render a medical opinion that suffocation is one of the ways someone could cause the child's death without leaving obvious medical signs.

Conclusion

Both the medical and legal professions have made great strides in identifying nonaccidental trauma inflicted on children. This progress accounts for what appears to be an increase in the number of identified child abuse homicides. Sadly, however, there will always be some children who die of abuse that is never discovered. Children and society deserve investigators' best efforts to turn over every stone in cases involving any suspicion of the abuse of children.

Author

Rob Parrish
Chief Child Abuse Counsel
Office of the Attorney General
160 East 300 South, Sixth Floor
Salt Lake City, UT 84114
801–366–0510
801–366–0204 (fax)

Supplemental Reading

Child Fatalities

Anderson TL, Wells SJ. *Data Collection for Child Fatalities: Existing Efforts and Proposed Guidelines*. Chicago, IL: American Bar Association, 1991.

Combs DL, Parrish RG, Ing R. *Death Investigation in the United States and Canada, 1995*. Atlanta, GA: U.S. Department of Health and Human Services, Public Health Service, Centers for Disease Control and Prevention, National Center for Environmental Health, Division of Environmental Hazards and Health Effects, August 1995.

Current Trends in Child Abuse Reporting and Fatalities: The Results of the 1995 Annual Fifty State Survey. Chicago, IL: National Committee for Prevention of Child Abuse, April 1996.

Granik LA, Durfee M, Wells SJ. *Child Death Review Teams: A Manual for Design and Implementation*. Chicago, IL: American Bar Association, 1991.

Kaplan SR. *Child Fatality Legislation in the United States*. Chicago, IL: American Bar Association, 1991.

Kaplan SR, Granik LA (eds). *Child Fatality Investigative Procedures Manual*. Chicago, IL: American Bar Association, 1991.

Shepherd JR, Dworin B, Farley RH, Russ BJ, Tressler PW, National Center for Missing and Exploited Children. *Child Abuse and Exploitation: Investigative Techniques*. 2d ed. Washington, DC: Office of Juvenile Justice and Delinquency Prevention, 1995.

U.S. Advisory Board on Child Abuse and Neglect. *A Nation's Shame: Fatal Child Abuse and Neglect in the United States.* Washington, DC: U.S. Advisory Board on Child Abuse and Neglect, April 1995.

Child Fatality Laws

The following statutory publications are available from the National Clearinghouse on Child Abuse and Neglect Information, 800–FYI–3366, 703–385–7565. Each contains State and territory laws on the given topic.

Child Abuse and Neglect Crimes: Child Homicide.

Child Death Review Teams/Mandatory Autopsies.

Reporting Suspicious Deaths.

Sudden Infant Death Syndrome

National Sudden Infant Death Syndrome Clearinghouse. *Death Investigations and Sudden Infant Death Syndrome: A Selected Annotated Bibliography.* U.S. Department of Health and Human Services, Public Health Service, Health Resources and Services Administration, Maternal and Child Health Bureau, September 1991.

National Sudden Infant Death Syndrome Clearinghouse. *The Professional's Role in Sudden Infant Death Syndrome: A Selected Annotated Bibliography.* U.S. Department of Health and Human Services, Public Health Service, Health Resources and Services Administration, Maternal and Child Health Bureau, September 1991.

National Sudden Infant Death Syndrome Resource Center. *Sudden Infant Death Syndrome Research: A Selected Annotated Bibliography for 1993.* McLean, VA: U.S. Department of Health and Human Services, Public Health Service, Health Resources and Services Administration, Maternal and Child Health Bureau, May 1994.

National Sudden Infant Death Syndrome Resource Center. *Sudden Infant Death Syndrome Risk Factors: A Selected Annotated Bibliography for 1989–1993.* McLean, VA: U.S. Department of Health and Human Services, Public Health Service, Health Resources and Services Administration, Maternal and Child Health Bureau, May 1994.

National Sudden Infant Death Syndrome Resource Center. *Sudden Infant Death Syndrome: Trying To Understand the Mystery.* McLean, VA: U.S. Department of Health and Human Services, Public Health Service, Health Resources and Services Administration, Maternal and Child Health Bureau, February 1994.

National Sudden Infant Death Syndrome Resource Center. *What is SIDS?* (Information Sheet). McLean, VA: U.S. Department of Health and Human Services, Public Health Service, Health Resources and Services Administration, Maternal and Child Health Bureau, May 1993.

Willinger M, James LS, Catz C. Defining the sudden infant death syndrome (SIDS): Deliberations of an expert panel convened by the National Institute of Child Health and Human Development. *Pediatric Pathology* 11:677–684, 1991.

Death Certification and National Death Statistics

The following three references are available from the National Center for Health Statistics (NCHS), Division of Vital Statistics, Registration Methods Branch, 301–436–8815. General information on mortality statistics is available from NCHS, Division of Vital Statistics, Mortality Statistics Branch, 301–436–8884.

Funeral Directors' Handbook on Death Registration and Fetal Death Reporting. Hyattsville, MD: U.S. Department of Health and Human Services, Public Health Service, National Center for Health Statistics, September 1987. (DHHS Publication No. (PHS) 87–1109).

Medical Examiners' and Coroners' Handbook on Death Registration and Fetal Death Reporting. Hyattsville, MD: U.S. Department of Health and Human Services, Public Health Service, National Center for Health Statistics, October 1987. (DHHS Publication No. (PHS) 87–1110).

Physicians' Handbook on Medical Certification of Death. Hyattsville, MD: U.S. Department of Health and Human Services, Public Health Service, National Center for Health Statistics, September 1987. (DHHS Publication No. (PHS) 87–1108).

Organizations

American Academy of Pediatrics
141 Northwest Point Boulevard
Elk Grove Village, IL 60007–1098
847–434–4000
847–434–8000 (fax)
www.aap.org

The American Academy of Pediatrics publishes the following resources for professionals who come in contact with abused children: *The Visual Diagnosis of Child Physical Abuse*, a study guide and teaching slides that provide medical information about identification of physical child abuse and neglect; *A Guide to References and Resources in Child Abuse and Neglect*, a comprehensive manual on the medical diagnosis and treatment of child abuse and neglect; and *Visual Diagnosis of Child Abuse* on CD-ROM.

Missing and Exploited Children's Training Programs
Fox Valley Technical College
Criminal Justice Grants Department
P.O. Box 2277
1825 North Bluemound Drive
Appleton, WI 54913–2277
800–648–4966
920–735–4757 (fax)
dept.fvtc.edu/ojjdp

Participants are trained in child abuse and exploitation investigative techniques, covering the following areas:

* Recognition of signs of abuse.

* Collection and preservation of evidence.

* Preparation of cases for prosecution.

* Techniques for interviewing victims and offenders.

* Liability issues.

Fox Valley also offers intensive special training for local child investigative teams. Teams must include representatives from law enforcement, prosecution, social services, and (optionally) the medical field. Participants take part in hands-on team activity involving:

* Development of interagency processes and protocols for enhanced enforcement, prevention, and intervention in child abuse cases.

* Case preparation and prosecution.

* Development of the team's own interagency implementation plan for improved investigation of child abuse.

National Center for Prosecution of Child Abuse
American Prosecutors Research Institute (APRI)
99 Canal Center Plaza, Suite 510
Alexandria, VA 22314
703–549–9222
703–836–3195 (fax)
www.ndaa-apri.org/apri/programs/ncpca/index.html

The National Center for Prosecution of Child Abuse is a nonprofit and technical assistance affiliate of APRI. In addition to research and technical assistance, the Center provides extensive training on the investigation and prosecution of child abuse and child deaths. The national trainings include timely information presented by a variety of professionals experienced in the medical, legal, and investigative aspects of child abuse.

Additional Resources

American Bar Association
(ABA) Center on Children
and the Law
Washington, DC
202–662–1720
www.abanet.org/child/
home.html

American Humane Association
Englewood, Colorado
800–227–4645
303–792–9900
www.americanhumane.org

American Medical Association
(AMA)
Chicago, Illinois
312–464–5000
www.ama-assn.org

American Professional Society
on the Abuse of Children
(APSAC)
Oklahoma City, OK
405–271–8202
www.apsac.org

Federal Bureau of Investigation
(FBI)
202–324–3000
www.fbi.gov

National Center for the
Analysis of Violent Crime
www.fbi.gov/hq/isd/cirg/
ncavc.htm

Crimes Against Children
Program
www.fbi.gov/hq/cid/cac/
crimesmain.htm

Juvenile Justice Clearinghouse
(JJC)
Rockville, Maryland
800–638–8736
ojjdp.ncjrs.org/about/
clearh.html

Kempe Children's Center
Denver, Colorado
303–864–5252
www.kempecenter.org

Missing and Exploited
Children's Training Program
Fox Valley Technical College
Appleton, Wisconsin
800–648–4966
dept.fvtc.edu/ojjdp

National Association of
Medical Examiners
St. Louis, Missouri
314–577–8298
www.thename.org

National Center for Missing
and Exploited Children
(NCMEC)
Alexandria, Virginia
800–THE–LOST
703–274–3900
www.missingkids.com

National Center for Prosecution
of Child Abuse
Alexandria, Virginia
703–549–9222
www.ndaa-apri.org/apri/
programs/ncpca/index.html

National Children's Alliance
Washington, DC
800–239–9950
202–452–6001
www.nncac.org

National Clearinghouse
on Child Abuse and
Neglect Information
Washington, DC
800–394–3366
703–385–7565
www.calib.com/nccanch/

National SIDS Resource Center
Vienna, Virginia
703–821–8955
www.sidscenter.org

Prevent Child Abuse America
Chicago, Illinois
312–663–3520
www.preventchildabuse.org